The Antics of a Cat Named

ANTONETTE ANTHONY TONY

MONA BEHM

MILTON & HUGO L.L.C.
4407 Park Ave., Suite 5
Union City, NJ 07087, USA

Website: *www. miltonandhugo.com*
Hotline: *1- 888-778-0033*
Email: *info@miltonandhugo.com*

Ordering Information:
Quantity sales. Special discounts are granted to corporations, associations, and other organizations. For more information on these discounts, please reach out to the publisher using the contact information provided above.

Library of Congress Control Number:	2024906881	
ISBN-13:	979-8-89285-013-1	[Paperback Edition]
	979-8-89285-014-8	[Digital Edition]

Rev. date: 03/12/2024

INTRODUCTION

During the 1970s in Iowa, I lived with my parents who were beginning to have physical problems. My father, who was six foot three and weighed over three hundred pounds, started having problems falling down and not being able to get up on his own. He had polio in the early 1940s. The doctors told him he would never walk again. My mother was a small woman only standing five foot two. However, she had remarkable strength and stamina. She was the key to my dad being able to stand and walk again. She started having seizures and was losing her sight in the 1970s. I, being in my twenties at the time, had the responsibility of assisting them in their daily lives.

In the fall of 1974, my father had a massive heart attack while driving, leaving my mother alone. With her eyesight failing and her seizures increasing, she relied more and more on me. She managed on her own until I came home from work. However, I never knew what I would find when I got home. The house consisted of ten rooms and a full basement. The stairs leading to the upstairs, where there were three bedrooms and a bathroom, were carpeted down the middle with varnish on either side. Before my father passed away, he put railings along the steps, which was a big help to Mom as she began having less sight.

While sitting with my parents after work and on weekends, I made crocheted and knitted toys and dolls for the neighborhood children. I also made lap robes and blankets. One day I decided to make a beanbag–type chair, which was popular in those days. It was made cotton of material and shaped like a hamburger. There was the bun made of a light-brown material and a cream-color insert. The top bun was stuffed with cotton to puff it up to about three feet. The bottom bun was flatter but also had the cream-color insert. I sewed a piece of red material in the center of the cream-colored material on the bottom bun to make it look like ketchup. Inside the bun, I made removable parts—a hamburger patty and a slice of tomato that were both stuffed with soft Styrofoam that was stiff enough to keep its shape yet flexible enough to sit on with ease. On one side of the tomato, I sewed white- and cream-colored pieces of material to give the appearance of a slice of tomato with seeds. Then I crocheted a large slice of cheese, yellow yarn, which could double as a lap robe. Being five foot seven when I would stand next to the hamburger, it was about waist high.

Six years after my dad passed away, my mom had a seizure; and after ten days in the hospital, she passed away. I decided to stay in the house at least for a while. Unbeknownst to me, at about this same time in 1980, in a barn in rural Iowa, a mother cat gave birth to a litter of kittens.

iN THE BEGINNING

In July, I was sitting in my favorite chair half asleep when the doorbell rang. Upon opening the door, there stood a legal secretary friend of mine with a pet carrier. Behind her was a young girl holding a litter box and what I assumed were pet accessories. Before I could say anything, she smiled and said, "I thought you needed something to keep you company in this big house." I was stunned, to say the least. She opened the carrier, and out wandered a black-and-white fur ball. Thinking that was it, I leaned over to pick up the fur ball when I noticed a little black head with a white star on her forehead poking out the door of the carrier. She brought not just one kitten but two! The black kitten had been named Cleopatra, and the black-and-white one was Antonette—both females.

Here I was at the age of thirty-six, never having had a pet to care for before in my life and faced with an unknown future. I picked up the black-and-white kitten. Holding her against my chest and listening to her purr, I melted and could not reject the gift. I told my friend thank you, *but* if it doesn't work out, I would return them to her for placement.

4

ROOM FOR TWO

After my friend left, "we" proceeded to get settled in. I carried the litter box and bag of litter to the back porch/kitchen, the only tiled room in the house except the bathroom, but that was upstairs. After placing the litter box on the floor and pouring in the litter, I turned around to find Antonette and Cleopatra behind me. I went back to get the rest of the gifts, and they started to explore the area. The food and dishes were placed on the floor in the kitchen and filled with food. The scratching post and toys were also placed in the back porch/kitchen area. My idea was the two kittens would stay in that area. However, when I came downstairs in the morning, I found the two sitting at the foot of the steps waiting for me.

STEPS TO HEAVEN

It didn't take long for them to decide to explore the upstairs. The first six steps were quite a challenge—steep. However, with their claws, they managed to pull themselves up the steps that were covered with carpet except for a foot on each side that was varnished. When they managed to get up the first six steps, they sprawled out to rest on the landing before heading to the top. At the top, they had a whole new world to explore. Coming back down, they would slip and slide on their rear ends over and down each step. Quite a sight!

DEVILS IN CHARGE

On the first Monday after my roommates arrived, I left for work telling them to "be good." They both sat by the back door looking at me with mischief in their eyes. Upon returning from work and opening the back door, I was surprised to find dirt and flowers all over the floor and two kittens sitting there with dirt on their paws and noses with expressions of innocence looking at me. My mother had always told people she thought it was a waste to put fresh flowers on graves. So when she passed away, most people sent potted plants to the funeral parlor. Most of them were brought to my home to be planted. Not having time to plant all of them, I stored them on my back porch. It was my mistake to put the two devils in charge of the plants! However, I had no idea the fascination they would be for the kittens. Pots were upset with dirt and flowers all over the floor. There was dirt on their paws and even their noses! I was frustrated, to say the least, as I cleaned up the mess. The two innocent "devils" watched. Something was going to have to change.

WHAT'S IN A NAME

On a Sunday morning in August, I approached a vet during the social hour after church. I told him about the new additions to my family. He suggested I have them checked out and given shots. That happened the next week when he said both "girls" were deemed healthy. When the vet examined Antonette, however, he said, "What did you call this black-and-white one?" I replied, "Antonette," and he said with a chuckle, "I've got news for you. Antonette is Anthony." From that point on, Antonette became Anthony—Tony for short.

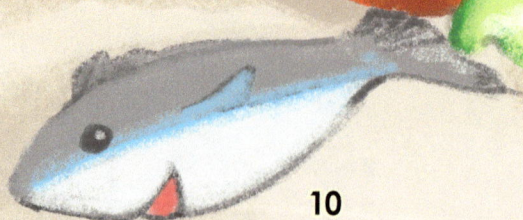

HOME INVASION

At this point, I was experiencing bouts of depression missing my mother, and remaining in the family home was difficult. This caused me to decide to sell the house and move. Since Cleo had not bonded with me, she was sent back to my friend for placement in a new home. Upon deciding to move to Arizona to be near my sister, there was a lot to do. I decided to take Tony with me.

Previously I had committed to having a Professional Legal Secretary (PLS) study group at my home for Labor Day weekend. Twenty-five ladies invaded our space that weekend to study and take practice tests. Every room in the house was used by the ladies including the floors. Tony sniffed around exploring their luggage. He crawled into bedrolls only to surprise them when they crawled in for a few hours of sleep. This was a nonstop, cram weekend. The test that was similar to an attorney's test to pass the bar exam was only a week away. The ladies had enough on their mind and did not need Tony bothering them for attention.

So Tony and I slept in my mini motor home in the backyard. The ladies studied and quizzed each other all night and took over the kitchen as well. Sleeping on the bunk above the cab of the motor home, Tony and I had a full view of the house. My eyes foresaw large utility and water bills along with a mess to clean up after they left. Thinking ahead, I had placed price tags on furniture and knickknacks. Then it was nostalgic, to say the least, watching the cars leave on Sunday heading to all parts of Iowa with furniture strapped to the roofs and rear of the vehicles. Come Monday morning, Tony and I surveyed the "damage." That's when Tony discovered some of his favorite sitting places were missing.

THE MOVE

Tony discovered a new game—hide in empty boxes and jump out to surprise me when I reached for another one to pack. The day came when the house was emptied out; boxes were packed in the trunk and back seat of the car as well as the motor home. A large mirror, shoe cabinet, and TV were just inside the back door of the house to be loaded the next day. Tony was getting frustrated. What happened to all his toys and favorite furniture—not even a bed upstairs!

The day before we left for Arizona, I left Tony alone while I went to the airport to meet my sister's husband who had volunteered to drive the car to Arizona. Tony would assist me in driving the motor home. After a night sleeping on the floor, the remaining furniture was packed in the motor home, and the journey began. Tony settled in the dashboard facing me. He stretched out with one paw hanging down just above the speedometer gauge. He wanted to make sure that I obeyed the speed limit that he marked with his paw—fifty-five miles an hour. We drove straight through from Iowa to Phoenix, Arizona, with only rest stops to stretch our legs and get a bite to eat. That's when Tony explored the motor home looking for "his" stuff.

MYSTERY OF THE MISSING GOLDFISH

I did not fully unpack at my sister's house in Arizona. She showed Tony and me the spare bedroom that became headquarters while I searched for a home and employment. Tony was confined to that room unless under my supervision since they had a dog, two children, and lots of things to get into. At night, he slept horizontally on the bed, and I slept vertically. He lay on his back with his hind paws against my side so he could push me back if I started to roll his way. One day the kids brought me a goldfish in a small round bowl. Fearing for the life of the small fish, I placed the bowl on the highest bookshelf in the room. It was in Tony's view as he lay on the bed. Upon returning from church one Sunday, I noticed the goldfish bowl was empty—no water, no goldfish, no mess! Tony was asleep when I entered the room. He woke with the look of a satisfied Cheshire cat on his face. The empty bowl was setting on the shelf where I placed it. The books next to it were perfectly straight. It's still a mystery—how did Tony take the bowl down, drink the water, eat the goldfish, and replace the empty bowl on the shelf without making a mess?

WAS iT WORTH iT

Our first Thanksgiving in Arizona was actually spent on the beach in Rocky Point, Mexico, in the motor home with three adults, two kids, a dog, and Tony. My sister and I took a walk down to the harbor where shrimp boats had just come in with fresh shrimp. We were loaded down with shrimp and a bag of small loaves of bread we purchased at a small bakery in town. After boiling the shrimp in a large pot, we all sat around the table stuffing ourselves. Tony just lay on the floor with his new friend Shinze, their dog, and watched.

Come morning, we decided to head back to Phoenix. Tony got in his position on the dashboard. The engine started up. However, the motor home did not move. We were stuck in the sand. At this point, Tony moved to the back couch so he could watch everyone placing boards under the back dual wheels and pushing. Before long, two burly young men approached us with shovels in hand. It only took a matter of minutes to dislodge us from the sand, and we were on our way back to Phoenix. At the border, Tony entertained the border guards from his position on the dashboard, distracting them as they searched for contraband.

BLOODY MESS

Just before Christmas, I was asked to house-sit for some friends of my sister. These people lived on Munds Mountain, a wealthy area in Paradise Valley, Arizona. Just to the right inside the front door of the house was a bedroom with bath that Tony and I shared. There was an indoor-outdoor pool next to a baby grand piano in the middle of the front room. I was told there was a cat on the property that I would have to feed, but not to worry, he probably would not show himself to us at all. Also, there was an Irish setter that required at least one walk a day.

The first morning I snuck out the door of our suite watching carefully for the cat. The dog was waiting with a leash in his mouth. He led me around the block waiting every so often for me to catch up. It was an uphill climb. Once back at the entrance to the house, he waited, but no second walk that morning. I had to go to work. I would go through this routine each day and spend my nights in the suite with Tony.

One evening after feeding the dog and cat, I squeezed in the suite door watching for the cat that had not let his presence be known to us all week. As I sat on the bed getting ready to change my clothes, I heard screeching cats in my adjoining bathroom. I found a large gray cat trying to get at Tony who was wedged in between the wall and the rear of the toilet. There was blood all over the floor and Tony. I managed to get the big cat out of the suite before surveying the damage.

The day before we started this job, Tony had his claws removed from his front paws due to a complaint by my sister that Tony had clawed in her hallway, damaging the rattan wallpaper. Not, knowing how long we would be staying at her house, I decided that would be the best thing to do since Tony was basically an indoor cat. After cleaning up the mess, I discovered the blood was from Tony's paws. He had spread his toes apart attempting to defend himself, and the blood came from his paws. He no longer had his front claws to defend himself. The other cat was probably shocked to see the blood when he didn't even touch Tony!

SETTLING IN

The end of December, I signed a contract to purchase our home after obtaining a job with an attorney. We finally received the keys to our house in February. Tony spent most of the first day in our new home exploring every room in the house while I emptied the car and the motor home. I had moved everything in the house—*except* no Tony! After not finding Tony in the house, I guess he had slipped out the door on one of my trips in the house unloading the vehicles. I walked up and down the sidewalk in front of my house yelling Tony. Naturally I attracted neighbors who helped me look for Tony. Finally giving up, I thanked my neighbors and with tears in my eyes turned to go into my house. Just then, one of my neighbors said, "Is that him?" as she pointed across the street. There sat Tony underneath the neighbor's car across the street. I yelled, "Tony get over here!" I started walking across the street yelling at him the whole time. Finally he slowly got up, came out from underneath the car, and sat there looking right at me as if to say, "Did you want me?" Since I kept yelling and pointing at the house, he apparently decided I meant business. He strolled down the driveway into the street, stopped in the middle of the street to drink from a puddle, and slowly walked right past me into the house!

I planted a vegetable garden—snap peas, carrots, radishes—and corn. When the corn started coming up, about three inches tall, I looked out my kitchen window one morning to see Tony casually eating my corn, which looked like grass at that point, one stalk at a time. That was the one and only time I planted corn!

A few blocks from our house was a park that had live music one night a week in the summer. When I got home from work, I put a blanket and snacks in the saddlebags on my '52 Schwinn bicycle and Tony with his blanket in the basket on the front. Then I pedaled to the park and spread our blankets on the ground, and the two of us settled down to listen to the music. Tony was a big attraction since everyone else had dogs that barked when they saw Tony. Tony would just look at the dogs with a smirk on his face.

SURGERY CHANGES EVERYTHING

One day I came home from work to find Tony lying on his back on my bed. His feet were sticking straight up. I lay on the bed next to him crying as I thought he was dead. Tony wasn't even a year old. After a while, he managed to turn his head in my direction and get my attention.

Upon taking Tony to the vet, I was informed he had a kidney problem that would require surgery. Tony spent two days with the vet and returned home with a shaved belly exposing his stitches and a cone around his head to keep him from licking his stitches. This is when Tony started sitting on the hamburger. He made an indentation on the top of the burger where his twenty-five pounds liked to lie. Also, he no longer urinated like a regular male cat after that, more like a human! He even acted human and desired human attention! When the front doorbell rang, Tony hurried to see who had come to see *him*. He would lie just inside the door on his back with his big white belly exposed, inviting petting by the guest. He assumed it was a nice person—not a burglar! Tony's favorite people food included fresh green beans lightly cooked. He did not like canned green beans—had to be fresh so he could sit on his chair by the stove to watch the beans cook. The other choice food was cantaloupe. He often climbed my leg as I stood by the kitchen sink cutting up a cantaloupe, trying to get the first piece.

Bonnie lived a block away. She was a cat lover and had cats of her own in the past, and when she saw Tony in the front window, she wanted to meet him. So one day Tony and I went to her house to visit. He sat on my lap, then on Bonnie's lap, and then jumped down and started walking down the hallway. I got nervous that he might get into something and followed him. He disappeared in an open doorway. I watched as he used the litter box, got out, walked past me, and got back on the couch next to Bonnie. No fuss, no mess!

When I had surgery, I came home with stitches on my midsection. It was hard for me to get into bed and out. I took all the pillows off my bed and used them to prop myself up on the couch. I put water, pills, and a cup of soup on the end table within my reach as well as a phone since that was before cell phones. Tony sat on the floor watching. I told him not to jump on me. After a while of watching me, Tony decided to get into his rocking chair that was nearby. From there, he could see if I needed help, and he could come to my rescue. He jumped into the chair, turned around a couple of times, and lay down. It didn't take long before he started slipping. When he sat down, his rear end was on the edge of the chair. It didn't take much before he fell on the floor. He sat there in a daze like "What happened?" I started laughing and told him not to do that anymore because it hurt me to laugh. It wasn't long before he got up in his rocking chair again—only this time he sat there looking right at me. That's where he stayed until I was able to get around.

PARTIES

Tony's first birthday was a big bash. I made invitations shaped like a cat and distributed them around the neighborhood and sent them to camping friends and others. The day arrived as well as thirty or more people. We played pin the tail on the cat, guess the number of gummy cats in the jar, and other children's party games. Everybody brought Tony presents. He sat in his rocking chair, and they piled their gifts around him. The guests—all thirty plus—enjoyed cupcakes, lemonade, and conversation. One lady, as she left the party, said this was so much fun; and I got to meet some neighbors too.

One afternoon there were a dozen or so people sitting around in my front room watching a lady demonstrate craft kits. She sat at a card table with a laundry basket full of kits beside her. After demonstrating a kit, she passed it around to the ladies and reached into her basket without looking for another kit. After a while, Tony strolled into the room and quietly slid into the basket next to her last kit. Everyone saw him except the demonstrator, but they did not say anything. When the lady reached down to get the last kit without looking, her hand felt the soft fur, and she screamed. Everyone laughed as Tony just sat there and looked at her as if to say, "What's your problem, lady?"

HALLOWEEN

Our church often had celebrations inviting members, their friends, and their neighbors. One Halloween, members of the church were assigned doors to various classrooms within the church. They were supposed to decorate their door and have treats to give to the kids as they trick-or-treated. Tony and I dressed like witches. He wore a black cape with a straw broom attached and a small witch hat. I wore a black robe and a witch hat. We waited inside the room until someone knocked on our door. When I opened the door, the little kids squealed in delight, "It's Tony!" not even acknowledging my presence. Tony was sitting on his chair and relished all the attention.

On another Halloween, my friend who had just had surgery was in a wheelchair, so we decided to go as a team for the costume contest. She was the patient. Tony sat on her lap with a white band around his belly. There was a red cross imprinted in the middle of the band. He wore a small white nurse's cap. I had a stethoscope, large glasses, a white coat, and a black bag. Patient, Nurse Nightingale, and I was the doctor. We won first prize—but naturally Tony got all the attention.

THE BOSS

A small cat started appearing at the back door looking for something to eat. When I came home from work, I would put whatever dry food was left in Tony's bowl out on the patio for the kitten. Tony watched as I put fresh food in his bowl, thinking, *This is a good deal.* He never made a fuss by the back door as he often did when a strange cat was in *his* backyard. Due to Tony's size—twenty-five pounds—I was leery to let the little cat in the house alone with Tony when I went to work. Finally when I had a Saturday at home, I opened the back doors, watching the cat slowly step in under the watchful eye of Tony. The cat explored the living room. Tony followed her. After a few tense moments, I was relieved to find Tony did not attack the kitten. He saw her (later named Camy) as his slave. She ate his old food. And later when he used the litter box, he would step out and stare her down until she covered his do-do. In the mornings, Tony would eat out of one bowl and then the other. Upon deciding which bowl he would eat out of that day, the kitten was able to step up and eat out of the other bowl.

Tony even tried to boss me around (before Camy). One night I got home late. Before I went to bed, I put fresh food in Tony's bowl because he always expected his breakfast at five in the morning, and I intended to sleep in longer. I made sure Tony was in the kitchen, closed the double doors to the bedroom, and went to bed, trying to get some sleep. Before long, the door started rattling. I looked toward the doors and saw a white paw sliding beneath the door. Tony was trying to jiggle the lock to open the door. I yelled at him to "cut it out! Go lie down!" It was quiet for a while. Then all of a sudden, *bang!* The doors flew open. He had apparently taken a run and pushed the doors open. Tony jumped on the bed, walked up to my head, and looked me in the eye for attention. My eyes were closed except for a slit, and I ignored him. The headboard on my bed was a bookshelf loaded with books. So he started taking the books off the shelf over my head—one at a time, they were dropped on the bed, and every so often he would pause and look me in the eye to see if I was awake yet. Not getting the results he wanted, Tony proceeded to knock each book off the bed with a loud thud. That strategy not working, Tony found a sheet of newspaper on the floor, which he chewed to shreds like a pile of litter. Tony jumped back on the bed to see if I was awake yet. Not getting results, he walked into the closet and began chewing on a plastic bag hanging from the clothes rack. The sound of shoes landing on the floor still didn't wake me; so Tony jumped back on the bed, stood on my chest, and bit me on my breast! Needless to say, I got up!

CAMPING CAPERS

I belonged to a camping club that camped every third weekend all around Arizona. Tony always went along. By this time, Tony had become leash trained. We took group walks to check out each new campsite. Tony walked too. However, when he got tired, he would just sit down—by that time all twenty-five pounds of him! I had to pick him up and carry him all the way back to the campsite. Before long, when the campers decided to hike, they chided me with "You know what will happen if you take Tony."

One morning I was told to get Tony and bring him to the campfire. They wanted me to put him in the empty woodbox, which I did. Tony sat in one corner, and a little, tiny field mouse sat across from him. Tony just stared at the mouse. Everyone laughed and said he should know what that is, having been born in a barn in Iowa. The mouse was released after fifteen, twenty minutes of Tony showing no interest in him. That was typical behavior for Tony. When visiting my sister's family, Tony enjoyed the attention of her children. One day the girl placed one of her pet white mice on Tony who was lying in the yard watching the kids play. The mouse walked over Tony's head and down his face to the grass without Tony moving!

34

We also attended state rallies where there would be five hundred or more rigs. At one such rally, we were parked in a section of the fairgrounds where there were ten rows of twelve campers. After we got parked, some of us decided to take a walk around the area. I left the back door open to get some fresh air in through the screen door. A lady sitting across from my camper said she would keep an eye on my camper when I told her Tony was inside. When we came back, I went inside to check on Tony. I looked at all his favorite hiding spots inside the camper but could not find him. A couple of us walked up and down a couple of rows of campers looking underneath and asking people if they had seen Tony. No results, so I went back to my camper, sat on the back bed, and started crying. Then I felt something beside me. Turning to look, I saw Tony sitting there looking at me with an expression that said, "Something wrong?" I had no idea where he had been hiding.

At one of the state rallies, I entered Tony in the pet contest. After numerous categories, they ended with small dogs. The owners were told to put their little dogs on a long table since they could not be seen on the floor. There were four small dogs, all barking and antsy. I put Tony on the table at the far end. He was bigger than the dogs. He lay down, tucked his paws underneath him, and stared right at the judges. It didn't take long before the judges stepped forward, presenting ribbons to the winners. Tony was given a green ribbon for honorable mention. The one who gave Tony his ribbon said, "Too bad he is not a dog!"

36

One campout as we sat around in lawn chairs visiting and enjoying the fresh air, a car drove up, and out jumped one of the campers' daughters along with a full-grown German shepherd not on a leash. Tony was sitting on his lawn chair with a leash attached. As soon as the dog noticed Tony, he took out after him, and Tony took off running toward our camper. Luckily the screen door was open. Tony dashed inside, dragging his chair behind him. The lawn chair folded as he dragged it and flattened against the outside of the camper door, blocking out the dog. Tony sat just inside the door still attached to the chair with his leash, looking at the dog and waiting for me to come to his rescue.

I often let Tony sit on the camper steps with his leash attached to the door. One time two roadrunners walked right in front of him, and he just sat there, not sure of what he saw! We went for one of our hikes, leaving Tony on the step. One of the men stayed at the campsite to keep an eye on things. When we came back, Tony was not on the step. He was not in the camper either. I sat on the step about ready to cry, thinking a coyote had gotten him. Then the man who stayed behind came out of his motor home that was directly across from mine. He was holding a black-and-white cat saying, "Is this what you are looking for?"

One campout, some new people came to check us out to see if they would blend in with our group. They had two small dogs that they let run out of their motor home without a leash. I told them all pets were supposed to be on a leash. They ignored me and let the dogs out one morning when

Tony was sitting on the step. They came up to sniff Tony. Tony did not like the dogs around him. He finally took a swing at them and hit one of the dogs, and the dog flew backward, landing up against a tree whimpering. The owners came running out of their motor home, and I told them to keep their dogs on a leash especially around Tony. He may not be a dog, nor does he have claws, but he has strength in his swing! Needless to say, those people did not join our group!

The church had an all-church campout every summer. When I pulled into the campground and stopped to ask where they wanted me to park, Tony hung out the driver's side window; and all the little kids came running yelling, "Tony's here!" Then when I parked, they all hung around the back door waiting for Tony to come out. They all wanted to hold him. He complied, allowing them to pass him around; however, he eventually looked at me for help; he was tired!

THE END

One campout, I took a lady with me who did not like cats, so I left both Tony and Camy home. Bonnie agreed to check on them. When I got home, Bonnie told me something was wrong with Tony. He would come up to his food bowl and just lie there looking at it. She said she tried treats, and still he lay there. Since it was Sunday, the vet's office was closed, and I had work to do, so I put Tony on the floor in my office with his favorite blanket so I could see if he needed me. We slept together that night. First thing Monday morning, I took him to the vet. After running a number of tests, he told me to take Tony home, and he would call me when he got some results. Upon returning home, I placed him in the corner of my office where he lay all day. It was around 4:30 p.m. when his kidneys gave way, pouring urine all over his blanket. I picked him up in another soft blanket and held him in my arms as I called the vet. I did not want to see him suffer, so I intended to ask where I could take him to have him put down. Someone from the vet's office was just starting to talk to me when Tony let out a big sigh and went limp. He had taken his last breath while in my arms. I said never mind and hung up the phone. Amid my tears, I called my camping friend and told her what happened, and she immediately came down to my house. By now, it was too dark to bury him outside, so we placed him in a large shoebox with one of his favorite toys and wrapped him in a blanket before placing him in the camper. My friend said she would be back in the morning. I cried myself to sleep that night. When my friend arrived, we dug a hole beneath my bedroom window. She placed a silk scarf around Tony, and we buried him in the sweet alyssum patch where he used to spend his days.